The Great Boys Book

Being your best through strength, courage, and kindness

Tom Fishman

Art direction and layout by Tom Fishman. Illustrations generated with assistance from ChatGPT-4o.

First edition.

ISBN: 979-8-218-67055-9

Published by Great Boys Books

For Gavin,
and every boy
who wants to be his best.

To be a boy is a very special thing.

And it's *especially* special to be
a Great Boy.

You might be thinking:
what is a Great Boy?

You might wonder:
am I a Great Boy?

Well, good news: every boy
can be a Great Boy.

Especially you.

All it takes is trying your very best,
every single day, to do
a few important things.

Here's how to do it.

A Great Boy strives to be strong.

Being strong allows a Great Boy
to do and try all the things he wants
to do and try, and to help the people
he loves and cares about most.

Getting strong helps you stay healthy and get better faster if you get hurt or sick.

Like a superpower!

Speaking of superpowers: a Great Boy uses his strength to protect others, especially when they are afraid or need help.

That's one of the greatest things a Great Boy can do.

Being a Great Boy does not mean being the strongest.

A Great Boy simply tries to make the body he's got as strong as it can be

And that's different for everybody.

What are some ways
you can make
your body
the strongest
it can be?

This is important:
being strong isn't
just about your body.

Great Boys also work
hard to have strong minds.

They're curious about our amazing world.
They ask questions.
They explore new ideas.

They learn from books and school,
music and movies, family and friend
faiths and cultures all over the world.

What are your favorite ways to learn new things?

A Great Boy uses what he learns
to form his own ideas.

In other words, a Great Boy
with a strong mind thinks for himself

And no matter how much he knows
about this thing or that, he
also knows there's
always more to learn.

A strong mind gives
a Great Boy one
of the greatest
powers of all:
discipline.

When a Great Boy has discipline, he is able to make good decisions for himself and the people he loves, even when it's hard.

A Great Boy with discipline might help his family by cleaning up after himself each day. He might save his money instead of spending it all right away.

Having discipline helps a Great Boy
stay calm and make good decisions
even if he becomes angry or
embarrassed or upset.

That's when making good decisions
can be the hardest.

Discipline helps a
Great Boy become
the kind of person
others can count on.

A Great Boy
strives to be
courageous.

Being courageous means
doing what's right, even
if it's scary or uncomfortable.

A Great Boy might speak up if his friends are treating someone unkindly, or invite someone in who's being left out of a group.

Being courageous can also mean
acting with honor.

When a Great Boy acts with honor,
he does his best to be truthful
and fair.

A Great Boy tells the truth
even if he might get in trouble.
He plays fair even if
it means he might lose.

One of the most courageous things
a Great Boy can do is admit when
he has made a mistake.
Everyone makes mistakes.

A Great Boy with courage and honor
will apologize when he's made a
mistake and do his best to fix it.

This is important:
courage isn't only doing
the right thing for others.

For example, it can take
a lot of courage to
ask for help.

Sometimes, a Great Boy
might feel sad or
hurt or afraid but he
doesn't want anyone to
know.

He might think
being strong means
hiding those feelings.

But that's not true. Everyone has those feelings, sometimes, and one of the most courageous things a Great Boy can do is ask someone he trusts for help.

Have you ever
had the courage
to admit a mistake
or ask for help?

A Great Boy strives to be kind.

Kindness turns a Great Boy's strength and courage into superpowers that can change the world.

Kindness starts with words.

A Great Boy says, *I love you,*
I care about you, and *I admire you.*

Just a few words can turn
someone's bad day into
a better one.

Kind words can let someone
know they matter.

Here's another way
Great Boys are kind:
they put themselves
in other people's shoes.

That's just a way of saying they try hard to imagine what others might be thinking or feeling.

When you put yourself in someone else's shoes, it helps you understand how to be helpful to that person.

Have you ever
put yourself in
another person's
shoes and imagined
what they might
be feeling?

Another way
a Great Boy
can be kind
is through his
service.

Service is spending time and
energy helping your community
become happier and healthier
without expecting anything in
return.

A Great Boy might help clean up
a park, collect food for people who
are hungry, or lend a hand to a
neighbor.

A Great Boy always remembers that he
is part of something bigger – a family,
a community, a country – and that his
service helps make a happier,
healthier world for everyone.

Yes, to be
a Great Boy
is a very
special thing.

Every boy can be
a Great Boy
by trying his best
each day—

To be strong,
to be courageous,
to be kind.

Especially you!